Contents

T0385966

Links to Abacus weekly plans

This information is for teachers who want to see how the Mastery Checkpoints are planned into the Abacus maths programme.

Autumn term 1		
Week 1	Checkpoint 1	Place value in 6-digit numbers
Week 1	Checkpoint 2	3-place decimals
Week 2	Checkpoint 3	Adding whole numbers
Week 2	Checkpoint 4	Adding and subtracting with decimals
Week 3	Checkpoint 5	Using letters for unknown numbers
Week 3	Checkpoint 6	The order of operations
Week 4	Checkpoint 7	Solving problems with measures
Week 5	Checkpoint 8	Subtracting whole numbers
Week 6	Checkpoint 9	Solving multiplication problems
Week 6	Checkpoint 10	Long multiplication
Autumn term 2		
Week 7	Checkpoint 11	Using negative numbers
Week 7	Checkpoint 12	Comparing and simplifying fractions
Week 8	Checkpoint 13	Finding volumes of shapes
Week 8	Checkpoint 14	Using formulae to find areas of shapes
Week 9	Checkpoint 15	Finding non-unit fractions of amounts
Week 9	Checkpoint 16	Using short division and remainders
Week 10	Checkpoint 17	Adding and subtracting fractions and mixed numbers
Week 10	Checkpoint 18	Using percentages
Week 11	Checkpoint 19	Multiplying and dividing fractions by whole numbers
Spring term 1		
Week 12	Checkpoint 20	Solving problems with really large numbers
Week 13	Checkpoint 21	Decimals with three places
Week 13	Checkpoint 22	Multiplying pairs of fractions
Week 14	Checkpoint 23	Mental multiplication with decimal numbers
Week 14	Checkpoint 24	Solving and checking multiplication problems
Week 15	Checkpoint 25	Drawing shapes and the vocabulary of circles
Week 16	Checkpoint 26	Solving addition and subtraction problems with large numbers
Week 17	Checkpoint 27	Common factors, common multiples and prime numbers
Spring term 2		
Week 19	Checkpoint 28	Calculating and interpreting the mean
Week 19	Checkpoint 29	Interpreting graphs and pie charts
Week 20	Checkpoint 30	Using a coordinate grid and transforming shapes
Week 20	Checkpoint 31	Finding missing angles in shapes and on lines
Week 21	Checkpoint 32	Solving long multiplication problems
Week 21	Checkpoint 33	Solving long division problems
Week 22	Checkpoint 34	Using formulae and describing sequences
Week 22	Checkpoint 35	Solving problems with ratios
Summer term 1		
Week 24	Checkpoint 36	Solving problems
Week 24	Checkpoint 37	Using equivalences between fractions, decimals and percentages

How to use this book

Mastery Checkpoints

The Mastery Checkpoints give you a chance to show how much you have learned about a key maths skill, straight after you have learned about it in lessons.

Each Checkpoint starts with a few questions for everyone to try. These are followed by some more in-depth questions in the Champions' Challenge section.

The title tells you which skill the Checkpoint is about.

Read each question carefully.

The Champions' Challenge section gives you more challenging questions.

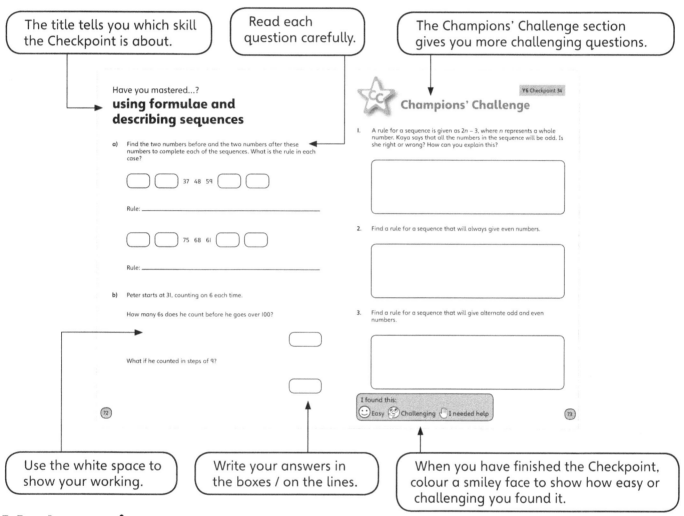

Use the white space to show your working.

Write your answers in the boxes / on the lines.

When you have finished the Checkpoint, colour a smiley face to show how easy or challenging you found it.

My Learning

On pages 82–87 you will find opportunities for you to reflect on your own learning: for example, challenges you have faced and how you tackled them, useful mistakes you have made and how they helped you to learn, and ways you might use the skills you have learned in real life. Your teacher will tell you when to complete each of these pages.

My Mastery

On pages 88–93 you will find tables that list the Checkpoint skills, and give you a chance to re-assess how confident you feel about each of them later in the year. Your teacher will tell you when to complete these self-assessments, for example, at the end of each half-term.

Have you mastered...?
place value in 6-digit numbers

a)   What is the value of the 7 in each of these numbers?

373 429

200 705

705 906

360 078

b)   Write these numbers in figures:

Six hundred and forty thousand,
six hundred and one

Four hundred and six thousand,
nine hundred and twenty

Six hundred thousand and forty six

Sixty four thousand and nine

c)   Write the answers from question (b) in order, smallest to largest.

1.

2.

3.

4.

4

Champions' Challenge

1) What number is 60 006 more than each of these numbers?

406 540

936 705

44 500

140 504

278 499

2) Which of these was the trickiest? Explain why.

_____

_____

3) Explain how someone could check your answers other than by repeating the addition.

_____

_____

_____

I found this:

☺ Easy 🤔 Challenging ✋ I needed help

Have you mastered...?
3-place decimals

a) Write these as decimals:

$\dfrac{33}{100}$

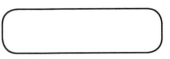

$\dfrac{603}{1000}$

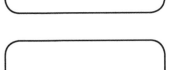

$2\dfrac{6}{100}$

$\dfrac{37}{100}$

b) Solve these:

$79{\cdot}8 \div 10$

$34{\cdot}362 \times 100$

$6{\cdot}57 \times 1000$

$3093 \div 100$

c) Write missing digits to make the sentence true:

$7\bigcirc{\cdot}\bigcirc \div 10 = \bigcirc{\cdot}5\bigcirc$

Champions' Challenge

1)   I am thinking of a number, it has six digits including a 3 in the hundreds place and a 7 in the tenths place. Give five possible numbers it could be.

2)   What are the largest and smallest possible numbers it could be?

Largest:

Smallest:

I found this:
😊 Easy 🤔 Challenging ✋ I needed help

Have you mastered...?
adding whole numbers

a) Choose two of these to add mentally and two to add using written methods:

19 000 + 23 + 16 000

65 788 + 18 407

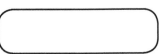

38 236 + 7678 + 46

38 + 2005 + 62

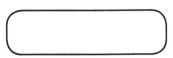

b) Two odd numbers add to give 20 000. Write two pairs that work.

Champions' Challenge

Find the mistakes in these calculations:

1)
```
    28 754
  + 36 348
    64 092
```

Correct answer: [   ]

2)   30 703 + 3307 = 33 100

Correct answer: [   ]

I found this:

 Easy Challenging ✋ I needed help

9

Have you mastered...?
adding and subtracting with decimals

The lengths of four pieces of rope were found to be as follows:

Rope A: 8·39 m   Rope B: 27·72 m

Rope C: 10·8 m   Rope D: 16·5 m

a)   Find the total length of Rope A and Rope B.

b)   Find the total length of Rope C and Rope A.

c)   Find the difference in length between Rope D and Rope A.

d)   Find the difference in length between Rope B and Rope C.

Champions' Challenge

The masses of four parcels are:

A: 3·58 kg   B: 2·805 kg

C: 0·55 kg   D: 1·25 kg

Peter says that Parcels A and C combined weigh 0·075 kg more than Parcels B and D combined. Is he right?

_____

_____

_____

_____

_____

I found this:

😀 Easy 🤔 Challenging ✋ I needed help

11

Have you mastered...?

using letters for unknown numbers

a) Find the missing letters in these number sentences:

$a - 65 = 90$

$a =$ [ ]

$2b + 3 = 35$

$b =$ [ ]

$7 + 12 + c = 40$

$c =$ [ ]

$d \div 9 = 8$

$d =$ [ ]

b) If $e + 21 - f = 43$ find at least three pairs of whole numbers that e and f could be.

$e =$ [ ] , $f =$ [ ]

$e =$ [ ] , $f =$ [ ]

$e =$ [ ] , $f =$ [ ]

Champions' Challenge

1) In a triangle, angle *x* is 72°. Write an equation showing how to find the other two angles, *y* and *z*.

_____

If *y* is 10° more than *z*, what numbers are *y* and *z*?

y = ☐

z = ☐

2) Write a similar equation for a quadrilateral that has one right angle.

_____

I found this:

 Easy Challenging ✋ I needed help

13

Have you mastered...?
the order of operations

a) Work out these calculations:

25 − 3 × 2

(30 + 18) ÷ 6

100 ÷ 5 − 3

7 + 4 × 4 − 3

72 ÷ (12 − 3)

84 ÷ 7 − 3

b) Add one or more pairs of brackets to this calculation to give the largest possible answer.

14 + 23 × 10 − 16 ÷ 2

Champions' Challenge

I) Use the numbers 4, 5, 6 and 8 once each. Use one multiplication, one addition, one subtraction and one pair of brackets. Write at least five different number sentences.

2) Write a calculation using the above rules to give the largest possible answer.

I found this:

😊 Easy   🤔 Challenging   ✋ I needed help

Have you mastered...?
solving problems with measures

a) True or false?

0·85 km = 850 m _____

3602 cm = 3·602 m _____

27·2 l = 2720 ml _____

83 g = 0·083 kg _____

287·3 km = 28 730 m _____

b) Peter runs eight 200 m sprints. Maya runs 1·5 km. Who has run the furthest?

_____

How do you know?

_____

_____

c) A jug holds 0·72 litres of juice. How many 100 ml drinks can be poured?

Can you explain why?

_____

_____

 # Champions' Challenge

Maya has a plant which is 15 cm tall. It grows 25 mm a day.

Peter has a plant which is 0·2 m tall. It grows 2 cm a day.

After how many days will the plants be the same height?

I found this:
😊 Easy 🤔 Challenging ✋ I needed help

17

Have you mastered...?
subtracting whole numbers

a) Choose two of these subtractions to do using counting up on a number line and two to do using written methods.

7125 − 3988

```
┌──────────────┐
│              │
└──────────────┘
```

12 000 − 8676

```
┌──────────────┐
│              │
└──────────────┘
```

69 561 − 28 342

```
┌──────────────┐
│              │
└──────────────┘
```

69 304 − 7583

```
┌──────────────┐
│              │
└──────────────┘
```

b) Write the missing number:

$$2000 - \boxed{} = 864$$

Champions' Challenge

Find three pairs of numbers that have a difference of 13 472.

In each case one of the numbers must be greater than 50 000 and one of the numbers must be less than 40 000.

$$\boxed{} - \boxed{}$$

$$\boxed{} - \boxed{}$$

$$\boxed{} - \boxed{}$$

I found this:

 Easy 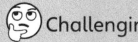 Challenging  I needed help

19

Have you mastered...?
solving multiplication problems

Use short multiplication to find:

a) 5672×9

b) The total length of eight pieces of ribbon, each 2·37 m long.

c) The change from £50 after I have bought six pizzas, each costing £7·65.

d) 3 is multiplied by 6 three times. Which of the following is likely to be the total?

396   648   1048

Explain your reasoning.

_____

_____

_____

Champions' Challenge

Drinks: £2·85   **Chicken Burgers: £8·28**   **Veggie Burgers: £7·45**

Dot's family buy 3 chicken burgers, 6 veggie burgers and 9 drinks.

Dan's family buy 7 chicken burgers, 2 veggie burgers and 8 drinks.

Which family has spent more?

_____

_____

How much more than the other family did they spend?

_____

_____

I found this:

 Easy Challenging I needed help

21

Have you mastered...?
long multiplication

a)   Set out and solve these long multiplications:

473 × 29

2905 × 36

b)   One week a factory produced 2478 boxes of coloured pencils. Each box contained 18 pencils.

Jamal said that he thought that was more than 45 000 pencils! Do you think he was right? How can you check?

_____

_____

Champions' Challenge

1) Using the digits 2, 3, 5, 6, 7 and 8, create two 4-digit by 2-digit long multiplications that will give an answer of more than 500 000.

2) Use the same digits to create a similar multiplication with the smallest possible answer.

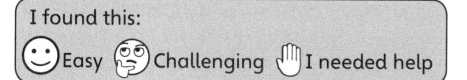

I found this:

☺ Easy   🤔 Challenging   ✋ I needed help

Have you mastered...?
using negative numbers

These are the temperatures in six cities one day in February:

London   2°C   Helsinki ⁻11°C   Sydney   17°C

New York 6°C   Glasgow ⁻1°C   Shanghai ⁻7°C

a)   Put the cities in order starting with the coldest.

_____

_____

b)   How much warmer is it in London than Glasgow?

c)   How much warmer is it in New York than Helsinki?

d)   Find two pairs of cities with a temperature difference of 4°C.

_____ and _____

_____ and _____

Champions' Challenge

I) Find the mean (average) temperature of the six cities.

The temperature in each city has increased by 2·5°C.

2) What is the new temperature in each city?

London:

Helsinki:

Sydney:

New York:

Glasgow:

Shanghai:

I found this:

 Easy Challenging I needed help

Have you mastered...?

comparing and simplifying fractions

a) Put these fractions in order, starting with the smallest.

$\dfrac{3}{2}$ $1\dfrac{3}{8}$ $\dfrac{12}{16}$ $\dfrac{15}{8}$ $\dfrac{5}{8}$

---

b) Which fraction in each pair is larger?

$\dfrac{3}{4}$ or $\dfrac{14}{20}$

$1\dfrac{7}{10}$ or $\dfrac{8}{5}$

$2\dfrac{6}{8}$ or $\dfrac{26}{8}$

c) Circle all of the fractions that are equivalent to $1\dfrac{2}{3}$.

$\dfrac{10}{6}$ $\dfrac{5}{6}$ $\dfrac{5}{3}$ $1\dfrac{8}{12}$ $2\dfrac{1}{3}$

Champions' Challenge

In each case, which is the odd one out?

1) $\dfrac{35}{20}$ $\quad$ $1\dfrac{12}{16}$ $\quad$ $\dfrac{14}{8}$ $\quad$ $\dfrac{32}{40}$ $\quad$ $\dfrac{21}{12}$

2) $\dfrac{24}{10}$ $\quad$ $2\dfrac{10}{25}$ $\quad$ $\dfrac{130}{50}$ $\quad$ $\dfrac{96}{40}$ $\quad$ $2\dfrac{6}{15}$

I found this:

 Easy $\quad$ Challenging $\quad$ ✋ I needed help

Have you mastered...?
finding volumes of shapes

The volume of a cuboid is length × width × height.

a)   Which of these three cuboids has the greatest volume?

     Cuboid A: Length: 9 cm   Width: 6 cm   Height: 7 cm

     Cuboid B: Length: 18 cm   Width: 4 cm   Height: 4 cm

     Cuboid C: Length: 7 cm   Width: 7 cm   Height: 7 cm

_____

b)   Which would make the best dice? Explain why.

_____

_____

Champions' Challenge

The volume of a cuboid is 900 cm³.

I)   What could its length, width and height be? Find three different answers.

_____

_____

_____

2)   If the length and width were the same, what could the height be? Find three different answers.

_____

_____

_____

I found this:

 Easy   Challenging   🖐 I needed help

Have you mastered...?

using formulae to find areas of shapes

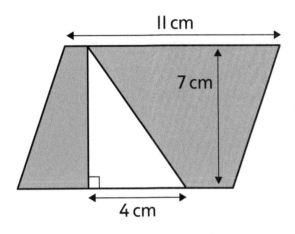

The area of a triangle is $\frac{1}{2}$ base × height.

The area of a parallelogram is base × height.

a)   What is the area of the shaded part of this shape?

b)   The area of a parallelogram is 54 cm². If its base is 9 cm what is its height?

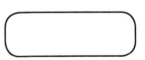

c)   The area of a triangle is 40 cm². If its height is 10 cm what is its base?

Champions' Challenge

1)   Peter says that if you double the length and width of a rectangle you will double its area. Is he right?

_____

How can you explain your answer?

_____

_____

_____

2)   Give some examples to show if he is right or wrong.

_____

_____

_____

I found this:

☺ Easy   🤔 Challenging   ✋ I needed help

Have you mastered...?

finding non-unit fractions of amounts

a) Find the following:

$\frac{2}{3}$ of 72

$\frac{5}{6}$ of 54

$\frac{7}{12}$ of 120

b) Which is greater and by how much? $\frac{3}{7}$ of 147 or $\frac{2}{5}$ of 155?

Champions' Challenge

1) $\frac{5}{9}$ of a number is 45. What is the number?

2) How many 7ths of 63 are equal to 36?

I found this:

 Easy Challenging I needed help

33

Have you mastered...?
using short division and remainders

a) Solve these divisions giving the remainders as fractions:

748 ÷ 3

9707 ÷ 8

b) Pencils come in boxes of 8. If there are 349 children in the school, how many boxes are needed for all the pupils to have a new pencil?

Champions' Challenge

I'm thinking of a number below 100. When I divide it by 6 the remainder is 5. When I divide it by 8 the remainder is 1.

1) What could my number be? How many possible answers can you find?

2) Find a number greater than 100 that gives the same remainders when dividing by 6 and by 8.

I found this:

☺ Easy   🤔 Challenging   ✋ I needed help

Have you mastered...?

adding and subtracting fractions and mixed numbers

a)   Solve these calculations:

$\dfrac{2}{5} + \dfrac{3}{15}$

$1\dfrac{5}{9} + \dfrac{1}{3}$

$1\dfrac{3}{4} + \dfrac{1}{6}$

$2\dfrac{3}{5} + \dfrac{1}{2}$

b)   True or false?

Adding $\dfrac{1}{2}$ to two other fractions always gives an answer greater than 1.

Champions' Challenge

1) Two fractions with different denominators have been added. The total is $\frac{9}{10}$. What could the two fractions be? Find two possible answers.

2) Subtracting one fraction from another with a different denominator leaves $\frac{1}{3}$. What could the two fractions be? Find two possible answers.

I found this:

 Easy Challenging 🖐 I needed help

Have you mastered...?
using percentages

a)   What is 75% of £96?

b)   What is 30% of £120?

c)   Which is greater: 60% of 200 kg or 55% of 300 kg? Why?

d) Which is greater: 70% of £150 or 25% of £420? Why?

_____

_____

 **Champions' Challenge**

A book has been reduced by 20%. Its new price is £12. What was its original price?

I found this:

😊 Easy 🤔 Challenging ✋ I needed help

Have you mastered...?
multiplying and dividing fractions by whole numbers

Solve these problems, changing improper fractions to mixed numbers or simplifying where possible.

a) Three children each eat $\frac{4}{5}$ of a pizza.
How much pizza is that altogether?

b) $\frac{3}{4}$ of a lemon is needed for a cake.
How many lemons are needed for 10 cakes?

c) Four children share $\frac{2}{3}$ of a cake.
What fraction of the cake is that each?

 **Champions' Challenge**

1) Arrange the digits 3, 4 and 5 to create a number sentence of a proper fraction multiplied by a whole number, like this:

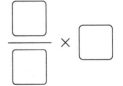

How many different ways can you do this?

2) What do you notice about the answers to your number sentences?

_____

3) Would it be the same if you used three different digits?

_____

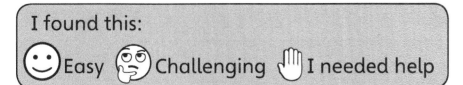

I found this:

😊 Easy 🤔 Challenging ✋ I needed help

Have you mastered...?
solving problems with really large numbers

a) Write these numbers in order starting with the smallest:

| 3 804 264 |
| 4 248 200 |
| 3 484 200 |
| 984 204 |
| 4 080 004 |

b) Round each of the numbers to the nearest 100 000.

3 804 264

4 248 200

3 484 200

984 204

4 080 004

c) Would 984 204 centimetre cubes fit in your classroom?

Champions' Challenge

I) In each of the numbers, how many times larger is the first 4 in the number than the second 4?

3 804 264

4 248 200

3 484 200

984 204

4 080 004

2) For each of the numbers, what number is 302 000 more?

3 804 264

4 248 200

3 484 200

984 204

4 080 004

How can you check your answer?

_____

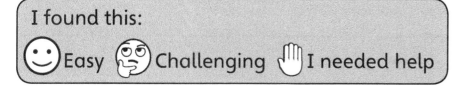

I found this:

😊 Easy 🤔 Challenging ✋ I needed help

43

Have you mastered...?
decimals with three places

a) Write these numbers in order starting with the smallest:

5·365   56·3   5·65   5·6   5·06   5·306

1.   2.

3.    4.

5.   6.

b) Are these number sentences true or false? Explain why.

8·047 × 1000 = 804·7

_____

23·5 ÷ 100 = 0·235

_____

9·6 × 100 = 0·096

_____

3871 ÷ 1000 = 0·3871

_____

Champions' Challenge

1) What number is exactly halfway between each of these pairs?

3·76 and 3·77

☐

14·583 and 14·589

☐

6·728 and 6·788

☐

2) I'm thinking of a number. I multiply it by 100, then divide it by 1000. I'm left with 8·63. Peter says the starting number was 0·863. Is he right?

_____

How can you check?

_____

_____

_____

I found this:

☺ Easy   🤔 Challenging   ✋ I needed help

Have you mastered...?
multiplying pairs of fractions

a) Multiply these pairs of fractions, simplifying if possible:

$\frac{1}{3} \times \frac{1}{4}$

$\frac{1}{6} \times \frac{1}{5}$

$\frac{2}{3} \times \frac{3}{4}$

$\frac{3}{5}$ of $\frac{5}{9}$

b) Maya ate $\frac{2}{3}$ of $\frac{3}{5}$ of a pizza. Sinead ate $\frac{1}{2}$ of $\frac{4}{5}$ of a pizza. Who ate more? Draw some pictures to explain this.

Champions' Challenge

1) Find at least one pair of fractions that, when multiplied together and simplified, will equal:

$\dfrac{1}{3}$

$\dfrac{1}{12}$

$\dfrac{3}{16}$

$\dfrac{4}{5}$

2) Gina says if you multiply together two proper fractions, the answer is always smaller than each of the fractions. Is this true?

_____

Can you explain why?

_____

_____

_____

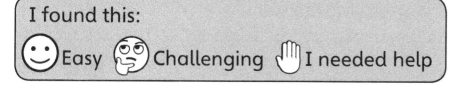

I found this:

☺ Easy   🤔 Challenging   ✋ I needed help

47

Have you mastered...?

mental multiplication with decimal numbers

a) Solve these using mental methods:

6 × 7·3

7 × 5·9

5 × 12·3

9 × 11·6

b) Which do you think has the longer perimeter, a regular octagon with sides 8·7 cm or a regular hexagon with sides 11·4 cm?

_____

Show how you know.

Champions' Challenge

Arrange the four digits 2, 3, 6 and 7 in this number sentence:

$$\square \times \square\square \cdot \square =$$

1) What arrangement gives the largest total?

What gives the smallest total?

2) If you change one digit, can you get a product of 73?

Have you mastered...?
solving and checking multiplication problems

Estimate then solve these problems:

a)   Which costs more, six tickets for the cinema at £13·45 each or eight copies of a new book costing £9·60 each?

b)   Which is longer, seven pieces of wood each 10·43 centimetres long or nine pieces each 8·76 centimetres long? Show how you can check using a different operation.

Champions' Challenge

Six friends travel from Acorn Wood to Beacon Valley and return the same day. They can travel by train or bus.

Train tickets cost £28·60 return. Bus tickets cost £13·45 each way.

1) Is it cheaper to go by train or by bus?

2) How much does the group save by choosing the cheaper transport?

I found this:

 Easy Challenging ✋ I needed help

51

drawing shapes and the vocabulary of circles

a)   Use a ruler and compass to draw a circle with diameter 13 cm.

What would be a good estimate of the circle's circumference?

b) Use a ruler and protractor to copy this shape. The sides should be the lengths shown.

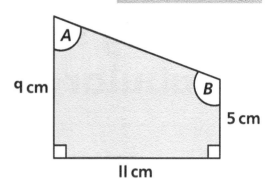

9 cm

A

B

5 cm

11 cm

c) What type of quadrilateral is this? What tells you this?

_____

_____

d) Without measuring, what do angles A and B add up to? How do you know this?

_____

_____

_____

_____

I found this:

 Easy Challenging 🖐 I needed help

Continues on next page

drawing shapes and the vocabulary of circles

Continued

Champions' Challenge

1) Draw an isosceles triangle with a base length of 9 cm and two angles of 50°.

2) What are the lengths of the other two sides?

_____

What is the size of the third angle?

⬭

3) If you doubled the lengths of each of the three sides of the triangle what would its angles be?

_____

_____

_____

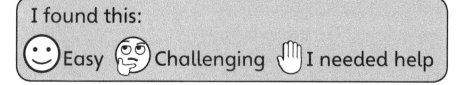

I found this:

☺ Easy 🤔 Challenging ✋ I needed help

solving addition and subtraction problems with large numbers

a) Set out and solve these using column methods.

4 340 283 + 792 670   452 372 – 72 086

The attendance at three football matches on one day was:
Rovers v. Inter: 45 620
United v. Hotspurs: 27 867
Athletico v. Wanderers: 9875

b) Use counting up on a number line to find the difference between the greatest and smallest attendance figures.

c) Use column addition to find the total attendance at the three games.

d) Is a TV reporter right saying that nearly 100 000 people attended the matches?

_____

Champions' Challenge

Jane adds three numbers together. The total is 100 255. One of the numbers is less than 10 000. One number is more than 65 000. None of the numbers have a 3 or an 8 digit.

1) What could the three numbers be? Find at least three different solutions.

2) Make up a puzzle like this for your friends.

_____

_____

_____

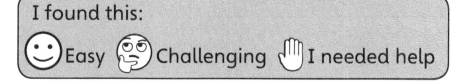

I found this:

😊 Easy 🤔 Challenging ✋ I needed help

Have you mastered...?
common factors, common multiples and prime numbers

a)   In each case, circle the odd one out and explain how you know.

Multiples of 6:   12   18   26   42   54

_____

Factors of 48:   2   3   14   24   48

_____

Prime numbers: 3   11   21   31   47

_____

Common multiples of 3 and 5:   15   30   35   60   75

_____

b)   In each case, give one more number that fits the criteria and one more number that doesn't. Explain why.

_____

_____

_____

_____

Champions' Challenge

1) Find two prime numbers that added together total 72.

( ) and ( )

2) Find all of the factors of 64.

( )

3) What other numbers also have an odd number of factors? Why is this?

_____

_____

_____

_____

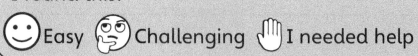

I found this:

☺ Easy 😕 Challenging ✋ I needed help

59

Have you mastered...?
calculating and interpreting the mean

House points in November
The 7 children on Blue Table scored 5, 6, 6, 7, 7, 8 and 10 House points.
The 7 children on Green Table scored 3, 6, 7, 8, 10, 10 and 12 House points.
The 5 children on Red Table scored 8, 9, 12, 13 and 13 House points.

a) Work out the total score and the mean score for each Table.

Blue total: ⬜

Blue mean: ⬜

Green total: ⬜

Green mean: ⬜

Red total: ⬜

Red mean: ⬜

b) Chan says that the Table with the highest total will have the best mean score. Is he right? How do you know?

_____

_____

_____

Champions' Challenge

1) There were eight children on the Yellow Table. Their mean score was 9. If Peter scored 7 and Mary scored 11 and no two children scored the same number, what could be the scores of the other six children?

2) Why is the mean a better measure of which Table did best than the actual total number of points?

_____

_____

_____

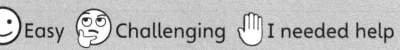

I found this:

😊 Easy 🤔 Challenging ✋ I needed help

61

Have you mastered...?

interpreting graphs and pie charts

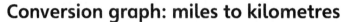

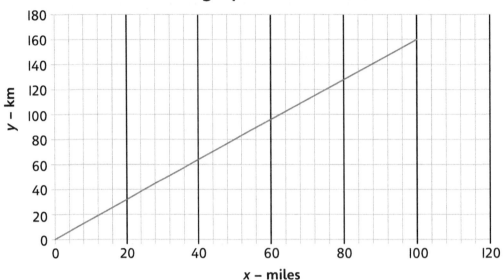

Conversion graph: miles to kilometres

Use the graph and pie chart to decide whether these statements are true or false. Explain why.

a) A journey of 60 miles is less than 100 km.

_____

_____

b) 120 km is a greater distance than 80 miles.

_____

_____

c) Travelling 50 miles is the same as going 80 km.

_____

_____

Favourite types of film - a survey of 400 children

d) More than 200 children chose Fantasy as their favourite kind of film.

_____

_____

e) 100 children chose Sci Fi as their favourite type of film.

_____

_____

f) The number of children who chose Horror is smaller than the number who chose Adventure.

_____

_____

I found this:

☺ Easy 🤔 Challenging ✋ I needed help

Continues on next page

interpreting graphs and pie charts

Continued

Champions' Challenge

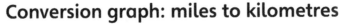

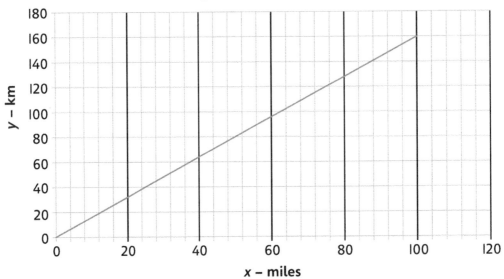

Conversion graph: miles to kilometres

y – km

x – miles

I) If the miles to kilometres graph was extended, which of these would be equivalent distances? (Circle any equivalent pairs.)

200 miles and 300 km

400 km and 200 miles

1000 miles and 1600 km

Favourite types of film - a survey of 400 children

2) Estimate how many children chose each type of film. What percentage of the children surveyed are each of these numbers?

Type of film	Estimated number of children	Estimated percentage
Fantasy		
Sci Fi		
Adventure		
Horror		
Comedy		

I found this:

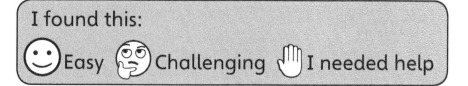

😊 Easy 🤔 Challenging ✋ I needed help

Have you mastered...?

using a coordinate grid and transforming shapes

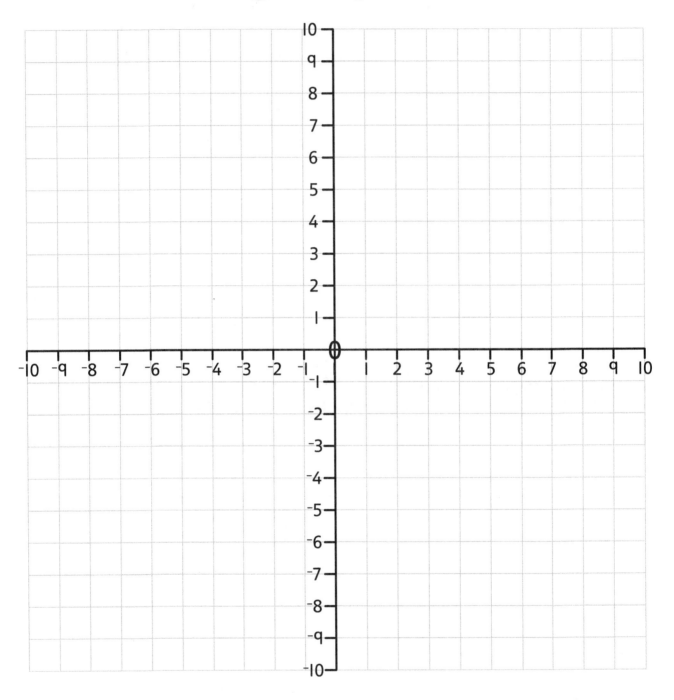

a) Plot the following sets of points on the coordinate grid and join each up carefully with a ruler and pencil.

Shape A: (3, 5) (8, 3) (8, 5) (3, 7)

Shape B: (⁻8, 3) (⁻3, 5) (⁻3, 7) (⁻8, 5)

b)   Describe the transformation of Shape A to Shape B.

_____

_____

c)   Now reflect Shape A in the *x*-axis and carefully draw the new shape. Label it Shape C.

d)   What are the coordinates of Shape C?

```
┌──────────────┐  ┌──────────────┐
│              │  │              │
└──────────────┘  └──────────────┘

┌──────────────┐  ┌──────────────┐
│              │  │              │
└──────────────┘  └──────────────┘
```

Champions' Challenge

I)   Plot and join up the points: (⁻10, ⁻8) (⁻5, ⁻6) (⁻5, ⁻4) (⁻10, ⁻6) and carefully draw the new shape. Label it Shape D.

2)   How would you describe the translation of the shape from position B to position D?

_____

_____

_____

I found this:

☺ Easy   🤔 Challenging   ✋ I needed help

Have you mastered...?
finding missing angles in shapes and on lines

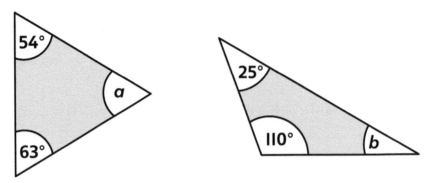

a) Find the missing angle in each triangle and say what type of triangle each one is.

Angle *a* is ⬚.   Type of triangle _____

Angle *b* is ⬚.   Type of triangle _____

b) In words, explain the rule for finding the missing angle in a triangle.

_____

_____

c) In a quadrilateral, the sizes of three of the angles are 75°, 110° and 55°. What is the size of the fourth angle?

d) What is the rule for finding a missing angle in a quadrilateral?

_____

_____

Champions' Challenge

In this diagram, angle *b* is 4 times larger than angle *a*.

What is the size of each angle, *a–d*? Explain your reasoning.

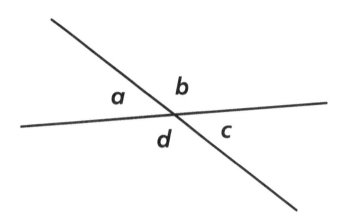

Angle *a* is [ ]

Angle *b* is [ ]

Angle *c* is [ ]

Angle *d* is [ ]

_____

_____

_____

_____

I found this:

 Easy Challenging ✋ I needed help

69

Have you mastered...?

solving long multiplication problems

a) Maths textbooks cost £8·55 each. The teacher needs to order 28 copies. Just by estimating, do you think that this will cost more or less than £300? Explain your thinking.

_____

_____

b) Now set out and solve the problem to find exactly how much the textbooks will cost.


```
┌─────────────────┐
│                 │
└─────────────────┘
```

c) The length of a field is 62·37 m. 42 children run from one end to the other. Just by estimating, do you think that altogether they have run more than 3000 m? Explain your thinking.

_____

_____

d) Now set out and solve this problem to find out exactly how far they have run.

```
┌─────────────────┐
│                 │
└─────────────────┘
```

Champions' Challenge

$$\boxed{}\boxed{}\cdot\boxed{}\boxed{} \times \boxed{}\boxed{} =$$

Insert the digits 0, 3, 4, 6, 8 and 9 in the number sentence so that the product is between 5000 and 6000.

Have you mastered...?
solving long division problems

a) Solve this division giving any remainder as a fraction in its lowest terms.

1304 ÷ 16

```
┌─────────┐
│         │
│         │
│         │
└─────────┘
```

b) 28 workers at a factory share equally a lottery prize of £8762. Estimate how much they each won, then use division to calculate how much to the nearest pound they each won.

estimate: ⬚

⬚

Champions' Challenge

I) In one week, the 23 children in Blue Class got 1056 House points, and the 26 children in Green Class got 1173 House points. Work out the mean score for each class, to two decimal places.

Blue class

```
┌────────────┐
│            │
└────────────┘
```

Green class

```
┌────────────┐
│            │
└────────────┘
```

2) Zainab from Blue Class said that although her class got a smaller total number they had a better mean average score. Is Zainab right? How do you know?

_____

_____

_____

I found this:

☺ Easy   🤔 Challenging   ✋ I needed help

using formulae and describing sequences

a) Find the two numbers before and the two numbers after these numbers to complete each of the sequences. What is the rule in each case?

( ) ( ) 37 48 59 ( ) ( )

Rule: _____

( ) ( ) 75 68 61 ( ) ( )

Rule: _____

b) Peter starts at 31, counting on 6 each time.

How many 6s does he count before he goes over 100?

( )

What if he counted in steps of 9?

( )

Champions' Challenge

I. A rule for a sequence is given as **2n – 3**, where *n* represents a whole number. Kaya says that all the numbers in the sequence will be odd. Is she right or wrong? How can you explain this?

2. Find a rule for a sequence that will always give even numbers.

3. Find a rule for a sequence that will give alternate odd and even numbers.

I found this:
:·) Easy Challenging I needed help

Have you mastered...?
solving problems with ratios

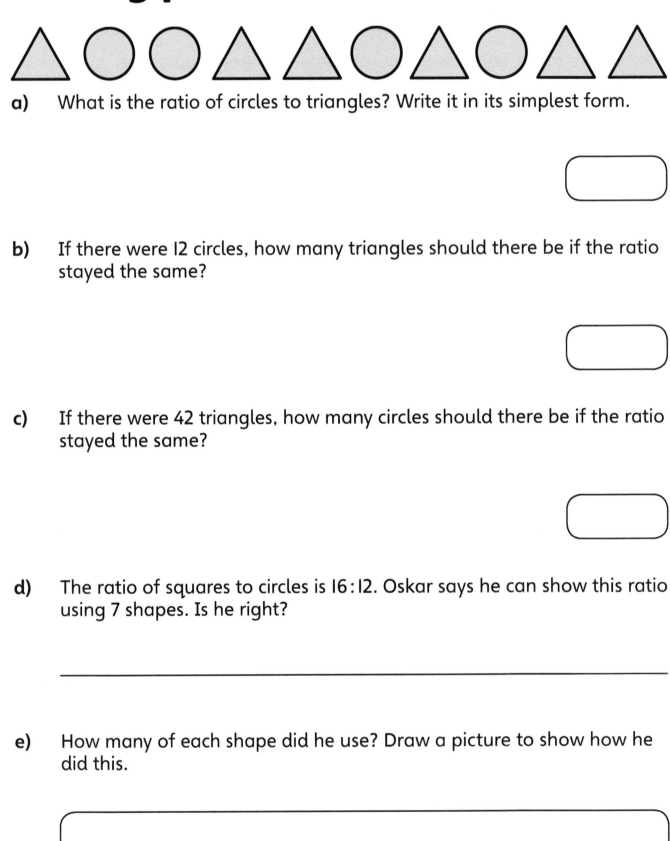

a)   What is the ratio of circles to triangles? Write it in its simplest form.

b)   If there were 12 circles, how many triangles should there be if the ratio stayed the same?

c)   If there were 42 triangles, how many circles should there be if the ratio stayed the same?

d)   The ratio of squares to circles is 16 : 12. Oskar says he can show this ratio using 7 shapes. Is he right?

_____

e)   How many of each shape did he use? Draw a picture to show how he did this.

Champions' Challenge

On a school trip, 2 adults are required for every 7 children.

1. If 8 adults are available for the trip, what is the maximum number of children that can go?

2. If 49 children are on the trip, how many adults are needed?

3. Make up a word problem involving the ratio 3:5.

_____

_____

_____

_____

_____

Have you mastered...?
solving problems

a) Mary is building a rectangle enclosure for her chickens. The length of the enclosure is 22·5 m and the width is 13·2 m. If she already has 30 m of fencing, how much more does she need?

b) I'm thinking of a number. If I subtract 32 from it and then add 17, I get 85. What number am I thinking of? Can you explain to a friend the best way to solve this?

_____

_____

c) Make up another problem like question (b) using at least two different operations.

_____

_____

_____

_____

_____

Champions' Challenge

1. Two numbers have a total of 78. If the difference between the numbers is 16, what are the numbers?

    ( ) and ( )

471 is exactly halfway between two numbers.

2. If one number is at least twice as much as the other number, what could the two numbers be?

3. If both numbers are more than 40 apart but less than 50 apart, what could they be?

I found this:

😊 Easy 🤔 Challenging ✋ I needed help

Have you mastered...?

using equivalences between fractions, decimals and percentages

a) Put these in order of size from smallest to largest.

$\frac{2}{3}$ 0·45   80%   0·7   30% $\frac{2}{5}$

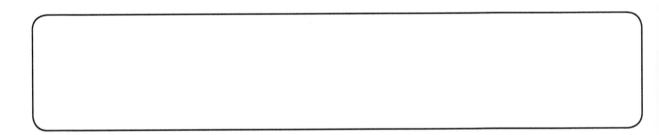

b) Which is heavier, $\frac{3}{4}$ of 84 kg or 40% of 150 kg? Explain how you know.

_____

_____

_____

_____

Champions' Challenge

A games console is in the sale in three different shops. These are the prices:

Games You Like   **Original price £250**   **20% off in the sale**

Terrific Toys   **Original price £300**   **25% off in the sale**

Market of Games   **Original price £280**   **30% off in the sale**

Peter says that the cheapest place to buy the console in the sale is the same place as it was before the sale. Is he right? Explain how you know.

_____

_____

_____

_____

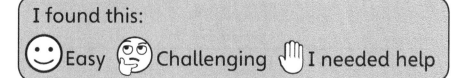

Date: _____

Things to find out

When you start a new topic, you will have lots of questions and things you are not sure about. Record your thoughts here.

What would you like to find out?

What skills would you like to practise?

What new skills would you like to learn?

What questions would you like answering?

Date: _____

Explaining my learning

Imagine your favourite celebrity is making a television programme about maths. As part of their research, they come to your classroom.

They have no idea what you have been learning about.
How would you explain your maths work to them?

Date: _____

My dictionary

There are lots of important words we need to remember when it comes to maths. This is your maths dictionary where you can record key mathematical terms and their meanings.

Give an example to help you remember each word. Use pictures, models, questions or word problems to help you.

Word	Meaning	Example

My challenges

As you learn a new topic, you will encounter lots of different challenges along the way. Overcoming these challenges helps to deepen your understanding.

What challenges have you faced during your maths learning? Why were these challenges important? How did you overcome them?

Date: _____

Real-life maths

What we learn in maths helps us in our everyday lives. Can you think of how what you have learnt in maths can be used in real life?

Think about any activities you usually do such as watching television, eating lunch, playing sport, or walking to school.

Real-life context	How I could use maths

Date: _____

Making mistakes

Did you know that we can learn a lot from making mistakes? They help us to move on with our learning.

Think about the mistakes that you have made and why they are important in your maths learning.

Mistakes I have made	Why they are important

Which of your mistakes do you think was the most valuable? How did it help you?

My Mastery

Colour a circle for each skill to show how you feel about it now.

Mastery Checkpoint	More help!	I think I'm OK	I'm the master!	Date
Checkpoint 1 pages 4–5 Place value in 6-digit numbers	◯	◯	◯	
Checkpoint 2 pages 6–7 3-place decimals	◯	◯	◯	
Checkpoint 3 pages 8–9 Adding whole numbers	◯	◯	◯	
Checkpoint 4 pages 10–11 Adding and subtracting with decimals	◯	◯	◯	
Checkpoint 5 pages 12–13 Using letters for unknown numbers	◯	◯	◯	
Checkpoint 6 pages 14–15 The order of operations	◯	◯	◯	
Checkpoint 7 pages 16–17 Solving problems with measures	◯	◯	◯	

Colour a circle for each skill to show how you feel about it now.

Mastery Checkpoint	Have you mastered...?	More help!	I think I'm OK	I'm the master!	Date
Checkpoint 8 pages 18–19	Subtracting whole numbers	◯	◯	◯	
Checkpoint 9 pages 20–21	Solving multiplication problems	◯	◯	◯	
Checkpoint 10 pages 22–23	Long multiplication	◯	◯	◯	
Checkpoint 11 pages 24–25	Using negative numbers	◯	◯	◯	
Checkpoint 12 pages 26–27	Comparing and simplifying fractions	◯	◯	◯	
Checkpoint 13 pages 28–29	Finding volumes of shapes	◯	◯	◯	

My Mastery

Colour a circle for each skill to show how you feel about it now.

Mastery Checkpoint	Have you mastered...?	More help!	I think I'm OK	I'm the master!	Date
Checkpoint 14 pages 30–31	Using formulae to find areas of shapes	◯	◯	◯	
Checkpoint 15 pages 32–33	Finding non-unit fractions of amounts	◯	◯	◯	
Checkpoint 16 pages 34–35	Using short division and remainders	◯	◯	◯	
Checkpoint 17 pages 36–37	Adding and subtracting fractions and mixed numbers	◯	◯	◯	
Checkpoint 18 pages 38–39	Using percentages	◯	◯	◯	
Checkpoint 19 pages 40–41	Multiplying and dividing fractions by whole numbers	◯	◯	◯	

Colour a circle for each skill to show how you feel about it now.

Mastery Checkpoint	Have you mastered...?	More help!	I think I'm OK	I'm the master!	Date
Checkpoint 20 pages 42–43	Solving problems with really large numbers	◯	◯	◯	
Checkpoint 21 pages 44–45	Decimals with three places	◯	◯	◯	
Checkpoint 22 pages 46–47	Multiplying pairs of fractions	◯	◯	◯	
Checkpoint 23 pages 48–49	Mental multiplication with decimal numbers	◯	◯	◯	
Checkpoint 24 pages 50–51	Solving and checking multiplication problems	◯	◯	◯	
Checkpoint 25 pages 52–55	Drawing shapes and the vocabulary of circles	◯	◯	◯	

My Mastery

Colour a circle for each skill to show how you feel about it now.

Mastery Checkpoint	Have you mastered...?	More help!	I think I'm OK	I'm the master!	Date
Checkpoint 26 pages 56–57	Solving addition and subtraction problems with large numbers	◯	◯	◯	
Checkpoint 27 pages 58–59	Common factors, common multiples and prime numbers	◯	◯	◯	
Checkpoint 28 pages 60–61	Calculating and interpreting the mean	◯	◯	◯	
Checkpoint 29 pages 62–65	Interpreting graphs and pie charts	◯	◯	◯	
Checkpoint 30 pages 66–67	Using a coordinate grid and transforming shapes	◯	◯	◯	
Checkpoint 31 pages 68–69	Finding missing angles in shapes and on lines	◯	◯	◯	

Colour a circle for each skill to show how you feel about it now.

Mastery Checkpoint	Have you mastered...?	More help!	I think I'm OK	I'm the master!	Date
Checkpoint 32 pages 70–71	Solving long multiplication problems	◯	◯	◯	
Checkpoint 33 pages 72–73	Solving long division problems	◯	◯	◯	
Checkpoint 34 pages 74–75	Using formulae and describing sequences	◯	◯	◯	
Checkpoint 35 pages 76–77	Solving problems with ratios	◯	◯	◯	
Checkpoint 36 pages 78–79	Solving problems	◯	◯	◯	
Checkpoint 37 pages 80–81	Using equivalences between fractions, decimals and percentages	◯	◯	◯	

Checkpoints ordered by curriculum domain

Number – number and place value		
Checkpoint I	Place value in 6-digit numbers	4–5
Checkpoint II	Using negative numbers	24–25
Checkpoint 20	Solving problems with really large numbers	42–43

Number – addition, subtraction, multiplication and division		
Checkpoint 3	Adding whole numbers	8–9
Checkpoint 6	The order of operations	14–15
Checkpoint 8	Subtracting whole numbers	18–19
Checkpoint 9	Solving multiplication problems	20–21
Checkpoint 10	Long multiplication	22–23
Checkpoint 16	Using short division and remainders	34–35
Checkpoint 26	Solving addition and subtraction problems with large numbers	56–57
Checkpoint 27	Common factors, common multiples and prime numbers	58–59
Checkpoint 32	Solving long multiplication problems	70–71
Checkpoint 33*	Solving long division problems	72–73
Checkpoint 36	Solving problems	78–79

Number – fractions (including decimals and percentages)		
Checkpoint 2	3-place decimals	6–7
Checkpoint 4*	Adding and subtracting with decimals	10–11
Checkpoint 12	Comparing and simplifying fractions	26–27
Checkpoint 15	Finding non-unit fractions of amounts	32–33
Checkpoint 17	Adding and subtracting fractions and mixed numbers	36–37
Checkpoint 18	Using percentages	38–39
Checkpoint 19	Multiplying and dividing fractions by whole numbers	40–41
Checkpoint 21	Decimals with three places	44–45
Checkpoint 22	Multiplying pairs of fractions	46–47
Checkpoint 23	Mental multiplication with decimal numbers	48–49
Checkpoint 24	Solving and checking multiplication problems	50–51
Checkpoint 33*	Solving long division problems	72–73
Checkpoint 37*	Using equivalences between fractions, decimals and percentages	80–81

Ratio and proportion		
Checkpoint 35	Solving problems with ratios	76–77
Checkpoint 37*	Using equivalences between fractions, decimals and percentages	80–81

Algebra		
Checkpoint 5	Using letters for unknown numbers	12–13
Checkpoint 34	Using formulae and describing sequences	74–75

Measurement		
Checkpoint 4*	Adding and subtracting with decimals	10–11
Checkpoint 7	Solving problems with measures	16–17
Checkpoint 13	Finding volumes of shapes	28–29
Checkpoint 14	Using formulae to find areas of shapes	30–31

Geometry – properties of shapes		
Checkpoint 25	Drawing shapes and the vocabulary of circles	52–55
Checkpoint 31	Finding missing angles in shapes and on lines	68–69

Geometry – position and direction		
Checkpoint 30	Using a coordinate grid and transforming shapes	66–67

Statistics		
Checkpoint 28	Calculating and interpreting the mean	60–61
Checkpoint 29	Interpreting graphs and pie charts	62–65

*These Checkpoints fall under more than one domain.